How the Settlers Lived

How the Settlers Lived

George and Ellen Laycock

Illustrated by Alexander Farquharson

David McKay Company, Inc.

NEW YORK

Library of Congress Cataloging in Publication Data

Laycock, George.
  How the settlers lived.

        Includes index.
        SUMMARY: Describes the living conditions, homes,
  clothes, and recreation of early Western settlers.
        1. Frontier and pioneer life—The West—Juvenile
  literature. 2. The West—Social life and customs
  —Juvenile literature. 3. Pioneers—The West—
  Juvenile literature. [1. Frontier and pioneer
  life—The West. 2. The West—Social life and
  customs] I. Laycock, Ellen, joint author.
  II. Title.
  F596.L43   978   79-5460
  ISBN 0-679-20684-1

                        8 9 10

MANUFACTURED IN THE UNITED STATES OF AMERICA

Contents

How The Settlers Lived

1

Into the Wild Country

The children knew that something exciting was going to happen. They knew by the way their parents spoke at the supper table. There was talk of a wonderful land to the west and of a long, long trip which would take them to that new place.

The wilderness waited beyond the mountains, inviting strong men to explore it, to clear its giant trees, and to farm its rich dark soil. Father promised there would be wild game to eat—as much deer, turkey, and buffalo meat as they could swallow.

The boys went to bed and dreamed of hunting with new rifles and trapping enough furbearing animals—mink and beaver and muskrat—to be rich.

Each member of the family would have to work hard to prepare for the journey. Many things to which they were accustomed would have to be left behind. So they packed up their clothing and cooking pots. Although father thought it might be better to use just wooden plates, like everyone else on the frontier, mother insisted on packing her pewter plates in a barrel.

1

The very earliest settlers who had gone west had walked there, and a few had traveled on horseback. They said giant trees stood everywhere, shading the earth until scarcely a patch of sunlight filtered through their leaves onto the forest floor. Because of lack of sunlight, there was not much underbrush, and the settlers and their horses could walk under the towering oaks, chestnuts, maples, poplars, hickories, and pines that made a dense canopy overhead. The trees had to be cut to make a trail for wagons.

The first settlers had followed game trails made by buffalo and deer. Indians, trappers, and explorers had followed those trails, too. The settlers stopped along the trails, whenever darkness overtook them, and made camp. They cooked their meal of venison or turkey killed during the day.

Before long, wagon trails were cut through the forest. Among the first vehicles along these roads were two-wheeled carts. Sometimes they were pulled by a horse, and sometimes the settlers helped to push the cart.

As the frontier opened, men with strings of pack horses hauled freight for the settlers. Two men could take ten horses. Each horse carried 200 pounds of nails, iron, or salt. The horses were tied together, the tail of one to the bridle of the next. At night they wore bells so they could graze and still be found in the morning. But when walking through the forest by day, their bells were muffled with grass to silence them in the land of the Indians.

When roads were cut through the forests, wagons could be driven over the rough terrain. A special wagon was developed for traveling over the mountains. The wagon bed was higher in front and in back to keep the load from sliding when the wagon went up or downhill. The wagon was also covered with a tall canvas. Beneath it, there was room for people to ride on top of boxes and barrels. But most of the time, the women and children who had space in the wagons climbed down and walked

A freight wagon.

along the rutted trails. Walking was more comfortable than riding in the bumpy wagons.

In addition to the settlers' wagons, there were freight-wagons on the trails. These, too, were heavy, creaking vehicles. They were piled high with merchandise to sell to settlers who had enough money to buy the wares. The driver rode on one of the horses or sat on a high seat at the front of the wagon, controlling his six-horse team with a single rein. When going down steep hills, the driver set his brakes and locked the wheels by running a pole through the spokes. Then he sometimes tied a huge log behind the wagon, to slow it even more and prevent his vehicle from running over his horses and crashing on the mountainside.

When a freight-wagon had safely reached the bottom of a mountain, another usually loomed in the foreground. Teams were often hitched together to pull the wagons up the steep slopes, one wagon at a time. Streams were a hazard, too, be-

A flatboat.

cause bridges were rare; wagons, teams and drivers were sometimes swept away on the rising waters.

A few of the early wilderness travelers left journals that tell us of their difficulties. In 1810, twenty-year-old Margaret Van Horn left her comfortable home in Connecticut, and traveled to Ohio to visit her cousins. Many times along the way she wished she had never left the East.

"We have come over two mountains today," she wrote one evening, "I have walked about eight miles. . . . I am so tired I can neither think or write. One misfortune follows another, and I fear we shall never reach our journey's end. The horses got mired, and we expected every moment one of them would die."

Along the trails, people opened their doors to travelers. Although few were turned away, travelers had to crowd in with the frontier families. People turned their homes into taverns as the traffic grew. Those who stayed in taverns often slept in un-

comfortable beds in over-crowded rooms. "We were oblig'd," wrote Margaret Van Horn, "all to sleep in one room and in dirty sheets."

Margaret also wrote in her journal that one woman tavern owner predicted that Margaret would marry and stay in the West. Margaret's answer was firm. Within three years, she said, she would be returning because she had not the slightest intention of staying on the frontier. She was ignoring the fact that few who came to the frontier ever went back. Travelers joked that the reason so few settlers returned to the East was "not that the western country is so good, but because the journey back is so bad."

Three years passed, and Margaret Van Horn did not return. Instead, she did what she had sworn never to do: she married and settled down in Ohio, where she lived out her life and reared thirteen children.

Rivers to the West became highways. Settlers arriving at Pittsburgh, where the Ohio River begins, could place everything they owned on a flatboat and float westward on the broad, shallow stream. Boat builders along the river banks built boats of many sizes.

Sometimes, several families joined together and shared the expense of having a large flatboat built for them. These flatboats contained small, closed-in shelters for the passengers. As long as Indians were a threat to river traffic, the sides of the boats were boarded up to protect the traveling families from arrows or bullets.

2

The Log Home

A family in the wilderness needed, first of all, a shelter against the weather. Because settlers could not bring building materials with them, nor have them shipped, they had to construct their cabins from what they found in the wilderness. This meant building homes of wood—not sawed lumber, planed smooth so the pieces would fit together neatly, but rough logs, hewn in the forests.

For a few, there was not even time to build a cabin. If a family had traveled all summer, cold weather was usually upon them when they arrived at the frontier. When flurries of snow filtered through the dark, naked limbs of the towering trees, there was barely time to build a temporary shelter. Instead of a cabin, they built an open-faced camp—a lean-to, with the open side facing the fire.

When Abraham Lincoln came to southern Indiana with his parents, the family spent its first winter in one of these camps. This was also the kind of shelter used by some of the very earliest hunters who came into the wilderness. A lean-to was faced away from the wind, and its back usually consisted

A typical lean-to.

of a large, fallen log. First, the hunter or settler placed two forked poles in the ground to hold the front of the roof. A long pole was laid across the forks. Then, additional poles, placed on this cross pole, extended to the big log at the back. Next, the builder covered the top and sides with brush and mud to keep out rain, snow, and wind. Buffalo robes and other skins, as well as the builder's possessions, were piled inside the shelter. In front of the lean-to, throughout the winter, he kept a glowing fire of large logs, and the fire reflected its heat into the shelter.

More often, however, a family new to the wilderness had time to build a cabin. When properly built, it was a tight, weatherproof structure. In the beginning, log homes had been built on the eastern seaboard by early settlers. Then, as people pushed westward, they built log cabins in the deep forest. Later, those who went beyond the forest and into the prairie lands also built cabins with the logs of cottonwood trees that grew along the streams. If there were no trees, the prairie settler cut chunks of sod from the grasslands, stacking them to make the walls and roof of a prairie home, called a "soddy."

The settler had few tools with which to work. He had an ax. He had an auger for drilling holes for pegs. He also had a froe for splitting roof shingles. Some even had saws. Homes could be built with these simple tools.

His first cabin usually had a single room and a packed dirt floor. The walls were built of round logs that had not been trimmed or squared. The logs were notched at each end to lock them together. Often, there were no windows in a log cabin, at least for the first year or two. Then, if the settler could obtain glass, he would install the windows. If he had no glass, he covered the space with the thin skin of an animal or with oiled paper, so that some light could enter the cabin.

Even before the walls went up, a settler had the shakes, or shingles, ready for his roof. These were made of thin pieces of wood, split from a block with a froe and mallet. The froe was a heavy knife with a short handle. The settler placed the blade

A prairie sod house, or "soddy."

Making shingles with a froe and a mallet.

on the top of a block of wood and hit it with a wooden mallet and in the same instant pried with the froe. This split off a thin, flat shingle. An expert woodsman could turn out 2,000 shingles in one day. The woods chosen for shingles were those that split easily. Cedar, oak, and chestnut were favorites. If a cabin builder had no nails to fasten the shakes in place, they were held down with long poles laid across them. The ends of the poles were lashed in place with rope or strips of bark.

While a settler worked on the roof, his wife and children filled the spaces between the logs to make them draft proof. If the spaces were large, the workers forced sticks into them. Then they packed the cracks with mud and moss to seal them.

Fireplaces were made of mud or clay. After erecting a cabin, the pioneer had to remove a space in the wall for the fireplace. First he made a three-sided wall of small, split logs around the new opening in the house. The wall was fastened to the logs of the house with wooden pegs. Fireplaces were made of materials found on the land. Often, when the settler built his first shelter, there was not time to lay up a stone fireplace. Instead, using sticks, the settler built up the form for the fireplace around the opening in the end of his cabin. Then he went to the creekbank and returned with a load of clay, or he mixed water with clay soil. This was packed between and around the sticks until there was a thick wall of clay. Wood, exposed on the inside of the fireplace, was burned off later by the fire.

Another, and longer lasting kind of fireplace, was constructed by laying up field stones, if stones were available.

Some settlers, especially in the South, made the fireplace by building up layers of clay, mixed with down from cattails. The cattail down helped bind the clay together. These fireplaces were called "cat-and-clay." However, heat dried them out and cracked them, so they soon had to be repaired or replaced.

When the fire was lighted, blue smoke curled up through the chimney and rose into the trees. Now the cabin was a

This cabin has a cat-and-clay chimney.

home, a shelter with a fire, giving warmth and comfort—a place in which to cook wild game, corn bread, and pork.

After some years in a cabin, however, a family usually made plans for a better home. This would be a house, not a cabin—and there was a difference. The house might be a story-and-a-half or a two-story building. It would also be made of logs, but much more work went into finishing them.

The settler cleared and leveled the dark earth on which his house would stand. He sometimes placed rocks for the lowest logs to rest on. More often, the first logs rested on the ground and were called the sill. These logs had to be especially chosen because they were the most likely to rot and could not easily be replaced. Cedar or locust were best for the sill because they would last longer. White oak, chestnut, or walnut were also considered good for the purpose. Pine and yellow poplar logs were often used for other parts of the house.

The settler cut the trees with his felling ax, choosing them carefully because each row of logs had to match in size. The sill logs were usually larger than the logs used for the wall above them. Then, he dragged the logs behind his horses or oxen to the location of his new home.

The logs were hewed to make them flat, instead of round on the sides, so that they would fit tightly together. First, the settler marked the log with a straight line along the side he intended to square. Then a long string was rubbed with chalk and stretched along the log at the line where the builder intended to cut it. He held it down, then "twanged" it, to leave a chalk mark on the bark.

Next, the builder, standing on the log, hacked two-inch-deep cuts, at close intervals into the side of the log, with the keenly-sharpened blade of his felling ax. Then, using his broad ax, and moving along the log with a steady chopping action, he removed the wood between the cuts. When he was finished, the log was flat on one side. He then did the same thing on the opposite side. These two sides would be the top and bottom

Scoring and hewing logs.

parts of the log, when it was in place. And if the settler wanted a fancier home, he might square all four sides of his logs.

At last the word went out. Early on the day set for the house-raising, neighbors came from miles around. Men brought their axes and augers. Women brought food. The settler whose home was going up provided a barrel of whiskey. Throughout the day, the walls of the house rose higher and higher. It took several men to lift a log. When the weight was too great and the wall was too high for men to do the lifting, the logs were rolled up on poles leaned against the walls. When the walls were up, the heaviest work was done. Some who had come to help went home to their own chores. Others stayed for a dance and a party.

The log house still needed days of work, but the settler could finish it himself. He cut away the logs where the doors and windows would be, and framed the edges of this space with boards, fastened in place with wooden pegs. He made heavy doors of planks. The settler had no iron hinges, but he knew how to fasten the door on its frame without hinges. He sharpened points on both ends of the long plank on one of the edges of the door. Then he fitted these points into holes, drilled in the top and bottom of the door frame. Now the door could be swung open easily. It was fastened shut with a latch that could be lifted by pulling a string. When the string was left hanging outside through a small hole in the door, anyone outside could open the door and come inside. If a settler said, "The latch string is out," he meant that the visitor was welcome at his house.

The door of the settler's house, as well as the cabin that had preceded it, had a strong bar that could be dropped into place to lock it from the inside.

After finishing the doors and windows and putting in a puncheon floor made of hewn logs, the log house might be white-washed on the inside, making it much brighter and more cheerful.

3

Inside the Home

As soon as they had finished building their cabins, early settlers had to build their furniture. A log slab, and four sturdy poles for legs made a table. Three-legged stools were also made of log slabs.

Wooden pegs were driven into the wall, and boards were laid across them to make shelves for a cupboard. If the settler's wife had pewter plates, she usually set them on edge on the top shelf. The men whittled out spoons and wooden plates, called "trenchers." They called the bowls they made "porringers," because they ate so much porridge from them.

The settlers drove pegs into the wall to support one side of a bed, and made legs for the other side. Boards or rope held the mattresses. In the early days, bed ticks, similar to large sacks, were stuffed with leaves, shredded corn husks or straw for mattresses. In the South, settlers gathered Spanish moss for their beds. Later, the pioneer women prized their flocks of geese for their feathers, which were stuffed into ticks. Goose down mat-

tresses made the softest, warmest beds of all. Each morning, the feather tick was shaken and fluffed up to redistribute the feathers.

Pegs were also driven into the wall so that clothing could be hung. And two pegs were put up over the fireplace or beside the door for the long rifle.

The fireplace was the heart of a settler's home. Not only did it provide warmth on wintry days, but all the settler's food was cooked over the fireplace's glowing coals. The settler's family made sure that the fire burned night and day, summer and winter, for there were no matches in pioneer days. Phosphorous matches were not made in the United States until 1836, and even after that they were not available widely on the frontier.

The settlers used flint and steel to start a fire. The flint, a very hard stone, was struck against a small piece of metal and this made sparks. The fire maker also needed tinder, an old rag, or a piece of frayed rope to catch the sparks. Many times he would have nothing but dry leaves or grass in which to start a tiny flame. He cupped his hand around the flame to keep the wind from blowing it out, and leaned forward anxiously to blow on just the right spot. As the fire caught, dry twigs and sticks were slowly fed into it until the fire was blazing. It sometimes took as long as half an hour to get a fire going.

If his fire went out, and a settler had a neighbor a mile or so away, he might send one of his children to borrow coals to start a new fire. The child carried the burning coals in a fire pan, a metal utensil with a long handle.

Because fire was vital and difficult to start, a family always kept an ample supply of firewood, chopped and stacked, near the cabin. Splinters were also kept near the fireplace for lighting the homeowner's pipe in the evening.

The earliest of all lights used in pioneer cabins were lard lamps and pine knots. Pine knots were lit in the fireplace and set upon the hearth. After hogs had been butchered, part of the

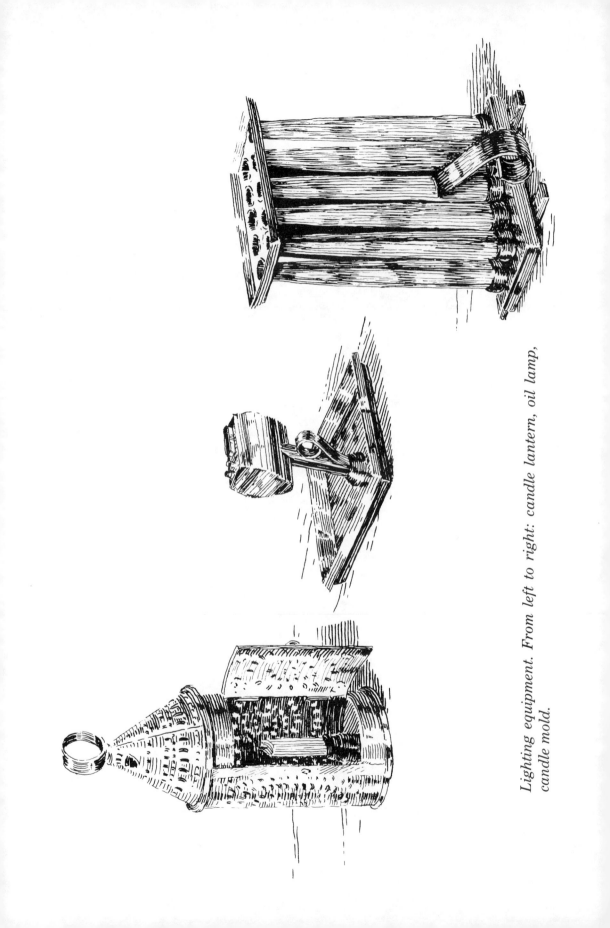

Lighting equipment. From left to right: candle lantern, oil lamp, candle mold.

lard, or the fat of the hog, became fuel for lamps. The lard lamp was called a "slut." A strip of rag, for a wick, was stuck into a dish of lard and lighted from the fire with a splinter. The slut made a smoky yellow flame.

These lamps were soon replaced by candles, which the pioneers made of tallow, the fat from butchered beef mixed with beeswax. They hung strings for wicks from a short pole suspended above melted tallow. Then the wicks were repeatedly dipped into the tallow and allowed to dry. Later, candles were made in metal molds. Strings were hung in the molds for wicks, and melted tallow was poured around the wicks to harden.

The settlers themselves produced almost everything they needed to live. But once in a while they had to travel ten or twenty miles, on foot or on horseback, to the nearest settlement with a store. At first, settlers might have nothing more than furs to trade for their needs. But when they began to raise domestic animals, they would trade butter, cheese, and ham for such items as sugar, coffee, tea, chocolate, and tobacco.

The pioneers brought seeds west with them. They grew corn, squash, pumpkins, parsnips, carrots, peas, beans, turnips, cabbage, and melons. And many settlers brought roots of young apple trees. One of the first things they did was to plant an apple orchard.

The apple orchard provided the pioneers with cider, apple sauce, apple butter, pies, and baked apples. They also dried apples so they could enjoy apple pie in the winter time. The settler's wife and daughters peeled, cored, and quartered the apples. They then strung the pieces on heavy black thread and hung them on racks in the sun until the juices had evaporated and the apples had dried. Or they sliced the apples and placed single layers of them in large flat baskets, that were set out in the sun or hung from the ceiling near the fireplace. Pumpkins were also cut up and dried in this way.

The settlers found the fruit of the persimmon tree very bitter, but the Indians taught them to wait until after the first

The interior of a typical country store.

frost to pick the fruit. Then they made preserves with them. They also dried persimmons and pounded them into a flour, which they used to make bread and pudding.

The most common sweetener the settlers used came from sugar maple trees in early spring, when the sap was running. The men bored holes through the bark of the trees, and made spouts from sumac branches with the pith burned out. These spouts were driven into the holes, and wooden buckets were set under the spouts to catch the sap as it dripped down. The buckets had to be emptied into large kettles. Then the settlers started fires under the kettles to boil the sap. The entire family, and sometimes neighbors, too, gathered together at maple sugaring time, keeping the fires going and occasionally stirring the syrup with a long wooden spoon. Children filled bowls with snow and poured the new maple syrup over it for a special treat.

The first batches of syrup were poured into boxes with dividers, so that the syrup would harden into cakes of maple sugar. Other syrup was stored in barrels and drawn off by spigots. This syrup was used all through the year on griddlecakes and cornmeal mush and for cooking.

Another sweetener the settlers often used was honey. Wild bees established their colonies in hollow trees deep in the forests, and the settler became expert in tracking them to where their honey was stored. To find a bee tree, he watched the bees as they gathered nectar. He saw the direction of their flight as they headed back to their colony, and he followed them. When he found the tree, he marked it. Then, in the early fall, when the summer's crop of honey was in the hive, the settler cut down the tree and carried the honey home in wooden buckets.

For the pioneers, salt was one of the most valuable materials—and one of the most difficult to obtain. Not only did they like it as a seasoning, but they also needed it for curing meat. Salt became especially important once people began raising enough hogs to send the pork to market. The Indians

Maple sugaring time.

knew where salt licks, or springs, were, and the settlers were quick to find them.

Water from these rare salt springs was boiled until only the salt remained. Beside Ohio's Salt Creek, for example, a long trench was dug, and two rows of iron kettles were placed above it. There were ninety kettles, each holding thirty gallons of Salt Creek water. Fires burned beneath the kettles, day after day, and their blue smoke mingled with steam from the boiling water, keeping a haze hanging over the valley. Within twenty-four hours, these rows of kettles could produce seventy bushels of salt. For each bushel of salt, the fires had to evaporate 600 gallons of water. Corn meal, added to the kettles, hastened the crystallization of the salt.

Salt production became a big business in the wilderness. Settlers rode on horseback many miles for a bag of salt. No one knows how many trees were cut to feed the fires that boiled the salt water. Salt production at Salt Creek and other areas on the frontier continued until the invention of the steamboats, which carried salt and other manufactured products, as well as passengers, to the West.

In the pioneer home, all cooking was done over the open fire on the hearth. The housewife had few pots and pans—usually only a kettle or two and a skillet. She stewed much of the meat she cooked, adding any vegetables she might have. The very earliest kind of fireplace had a lugpole stretched over the coals. Green wood was used for the lugpole because it would not burn. A kettle, filled with stew, was hung on the lugpole, and the stew simmered all day. If the lugpole burned, the dinner fell into the fire. When the lugpole was replaced by an iron crane, the settler's wife considered it a wonderful improvement. The crane could swing the kettle out to be loaded, and then swing it back again over the fire.

Large roasts of venison or bear were hung on a spit over the coals and carefully turned so that all parts cooked evenly.

Grinding corn.

Care had to be taken because hot grease, dripping from the meat, often popped and splattered.

The meat of young bears was more tender than that of old ones. The meat was sometimes cut up and threaded on long, green sticks—shish-kebab style. The bear meat was alternated with pieces of venison, duck, or turkey. When the bear grease melted, it dripped over the other pieces of meat, flavoring them and keeping them from drying out.

Indian corn was a mainstay of life for the settler, and it was eaten in many ways. As a porridge, hasty pudding, or corn-meal mush it was served as the first course of every meal. Corn-meal was cooked in water until the meal thickened. Then milk, butter, syrup, or gravy were added for flavoring.

The kernels were first scraped from the corn cob, then placed in a mortar and pounded with a pestle. The mortar was made by burning a hole in the top of a section of log; the pestle was fashioned from a block of wood, and a handle was inserted in the top. The person grinding corn bent the top of a young sapling over and tied the handle of the pestle to it. The springiness of the young tree helped to lift the pestle and eased the task of pounding corn.

Soon, however, mills were built beside rivers. The settlers carried their corn to the mills for grinding. A settler might ride ten or more miles to the mill with sacks of corn across his horse's back. But this was easier than grinding corn by hand.

The fine cornmeal was sifted out for corn bread. It was usually made by mixing the meal with water or milk and a little salt. The dough was formed into small cakes, laid on a flat board, and placed close to the open fire to bake.

Corn cakes were also called "corn dodgers," "corn pone," and "Johnnycake," depending upon the area of frontier. Sometimes lard or bear grease was added to the dough for flavor and texture. And yeast, if available, was used to make a lighter bread.

Shelled corn and the coarse pieces of corn left in the mortar were used for hominy, served as a vegetable. The hulls were removed by boiling the corn in lye water, made by running rain water through wood ashes. The hominy was then washed, time and time again, to remove the lye. After this, it was dried and stored for later use.

The settler needed a smokehouse for curing meat. He constructed this small building of logs. Cracks were tightly packed with clay to hold in the smoke that cured the meat. Smoking not only preserved the meat and helped to keep flies off it, but also gave it a special flavor. Freshly butchered and salted hams, along with bacon, and sausages were hung from rafters in the smokehouse. Then a small fire was built in the middle of the dirt floor. For days, the fire was smothered with chips of hickory and apple so there was more smoke than flame.

The settlers dug pits for root cellars, or built them in the side of hills near their houses. Here, they stored vegetables and fruits that kept into winter. A root cellar door usually faced away from the wind. The roof and walls were insulated with earth so that the temperature inside the root cellar would not dip to the freezing point.

A farmer might also build a small stone house over a cold spring that supplied the family's water. The water kept the springhouse cool in summer, and crocks of milk and butter were kept there so that they would not spoil quickly.

4

Battle of the Trees

The pioneers were the world's best axmen. They could swing a felling ax all day long in a steady rhythm, dropping trees almost exactly where they wanted them. But no matter how skilled they were, or how fast they chopped, trees still covered land they wanted for growing corn and hay. To the early settlers, the forests were enemies. The giant trees had to be brought to earth, cut up, and burned. Settlers chopped, while the smoke of their fires filled the valleys with a soft blue haze.

One method of land clearing, said to have put the trees down faster than any other, was slashing. In this system, the falling trees knocked each other down. A settler would wait for a windy day. Then he began notching trees on the down-wind side. Instead of chopping the trees all the way down, he chose one large tree, upwind, and chopped it until the wind blew it over. The falling tree knocked down the first notched tree and broke it. As that tree fell, it struck the next one. All the notched trees fell down, one after the other, until a whole field of them had been brought to earth. It was said that on a windy

43

day a good woodsman could knock down the trees on an acre of land.

Trees that were too big to be cut quickly were sometimes killed by chopping through the bark and the cambium layer in a circle around the trunk. The "girdled" giants stood, dead and leafless, throughout the following year, and summer sunlight warmed the soil for the first time in centuries. The earliest settlers planted their first crops among "deadened" tree trunks.

As the land was cleared, its value grew. Settlers who wanted dead trees removed from their patches of land sometimes set fire to them. After piling brush and grass around the base of a tree, the settler carried out a pan of glowing red-hot coals, and started a fire. The fire was spread to the next dead tree, and the next, until each tree became a spire of flame that sent blue smoke far into the sky. If the settler kept the tree burning long enough, all that remained was a pile of wood ashes.

Clearing the land of all its wood brought better crops than those sown among standing dead trees. Settlers thought it was better to clear five acres and grow a good crop, than to girdle the trees on fifteen acres and get part of a crop. Whatever the methods chosen, settlers worked for many years to clear their land.

After trees were cut down, there remained the work of cutting off the limbs and piling all the brush together. The tree trunks were cut into lengths for burning. Neighbors came in to help with the logrolling. Where a tree had once stood, its stump remained, and the earth was filled with its tangled roots. Brush, piled over a stump and set on fire, burned part of it away. But the rest of the stump had to be chopped and dug out. Where the sun had warmed the fertile forest soil, briars and bushes sprang up—almost overnight. This meant constant work for the settlers, keeping the brush grubbed from the ground.

The first year in a new home, the pioneer family might

Splitting logs for a rail fence.

clear four or five acres for a cabin and crops. More land clearing would go on for many years. The men became skilled at splitting long sections of logs for building fences and pens for stock. The rails for fences were ten or twelve feet long, and the favorite woods for splitting included chestnut, white ash, oak, and tulip poplar. Trees to be split into rails were cut during winter and split with wedges, made by driving a heavy wooden mallet fashioned of hickory. Some wedges were iron; others were made of tough woods, such as dogwood and ironwood.

The split rails were laid, end on end, to build a fence. One rail was laid on top of another in a zig-zag pattern, until the fence was four feet high or more. Some settlers also made fences by piling up stumps in a row high enough to prevent stock from escaping. Others made fences of field stones that, in some places, are still in use.

As the settler cleared and improved his land and its value grew, he found he could sell it for a profit. Along with the land, he was selling the labor and skill he had put into it. Some of those who took advantage of this opportunity, gathered their families and belongings and moved west or northwest, seeking new land to conquer.

These westbound settlers came to the prairies, but at first they rejected the grasslands. "Any land not good enough to grow trees," they said, "won't grow crops." But they were wrong. When they discovered that the prairies were among the most fertile lands in the world, the tide of settlers rolled on north and west.

5

Farming the New Land

The settlers made their own machines. "Were we obliged to run to distant mechanics, who are half farmer themselves," said one settler, "many days would elapse, and we should always be behind with our work."

By helping their fathers, many farmers learned, when they were still young, how to repair a wagon wheel, how to make a horse collar of corn husks, or a harrow from a log.

The farmer's wagon did a hundred jobs. He used it to haul grain to the grist mill for grinding into flour. He loaded it with hay to bring to the barn in summer. Or he put boards across the wagon for seats and took his family to church on Sunday.

Settlers also had high, two-wheel carts like those their ancestors used in Europe. These carts hauled stones for building stone walls or fences and transported logs from the woods. One end of a log was hung by a chain beneath the axle of the cart so only one end dragged on the ground. A team of oxen could then easily move the heavy timber.

In winter, if there was deep snow, the wagons and carts were replaced by sleds or sleighs. The sled hauled heavy loads.

The lighter sleigh, with thin, high runners, hauled families to church or to their neighbors, sometimes skimming over the snow at speeds of twelve miles an hour.

As the years passed, the farmer added to his buildings. To him, the barn was important—sometimes more important than the house. The barn protected his animals and his crops; on the barn floor, grain was threshed and corn was husked. Women, also, gathered in the barn to spin wool.

If newly cleared land was filled with roots, the plow's point would catch a hundred times before crossing the clearing. Each time the plow snagged on a root, the team and farmer were jerked to a halt. But once the fields were cleared of stumps and roots, the farmer could plow an acre or more a day. Behind the wooden plow, sometimes equipped with an iron point, the settler walked back and forth across the field, guiding his team by his spoken commands and by a line, running from the handle of his plow to the team that pulled it.

After the plowing, furrows had to be smoothed and clods broken. For this, the farmer made a harrow—often a log with some shortened branches. Or his harrow might be made of planks, drilled and pegged together in a triangle or square, and equipped with spiked teeth, instead of limbs, to break up the soil.

Corn was the most important crop. It was eaten by the settlers, and what was left was fed to the livestock. While the corn grew, the farmer sent his children to the fields to protect it from pests. They tried to scare off the crows, that marched down the rows, pulling up the plants. Some years, squirrels were a special nuisance; several times a day the children had to go through the field with noise-makers to scare them away.

At harvest time, corn was cut with a long knife. The farmer carried the stalks, an armful at a time, and stood them in shocks. Later, the corn was husked, and some of it was hauled to the mill for grinding. Every step meant more work for the settler and his family.

A plow with an iron share and a simple log harrow.

Farmers also planted rye and barley and, later, wheat. The seeds were broadcast by hand over a newly worked field, then covered lightly with a harrow. When the wheat was ready for harvest, the farmer came to the field with his cradle—a long, curved knife on a long handle. Rods extended behind the blade, like fingers, to catch the falling grain stalks. The farmer moved around the field, swinging the cradle in a steady rhythm. He then gathered the grain from the cradle and tied it into sheaths. These bundles were placed on their ends to form wheat shocks, which were later hauled to the barn.

Once in the barn, the wheat still had to be threshed, or separated, from the hulls and straw. This was done on the wooden floor of the barn. Wheat was usually threshed with a flail—a short hickory club, fastened by a leather thong to a long wooden handle. The settler lifted the flail over his head and brought it down on the grain. Finally, the grain was tossed on a blanket until the wind blew the chaff, or hulls away. This was a method used since ancient times.

As farms grew, forests disappeared, wild game became scarce, and the farmers' livestock became more important than ever to the survival of their families. Cattle, horses, and sheep needed hay for winter. In the early years, settlers cut wild hay in the marshes. Then, as they cleared the land, they began growing their own hay, and planting timothy—a tall, coarse grass.

When not working in the fields, the farmer had a backlog of important jobs around the house and barn. He had his hand tools, with which he made furniture, wagons, storage buildings, water buckets, barrels, spinning wheels, and sometimes toys for his children. He made, or bartered for, a variety of tools for woodwork: handsaws, augers, planes, hammers, and mallets. He often used a draw knife to smooth the edge of a door or window frame, or to shape a new spoke for a wagon wheel or a handle for his hoe. He also had a scorp—a curved knife on a short handle—for hollowing bowls from pieces of hard maple.

Using a wheat cradle.

Wheat was threshed with flails.

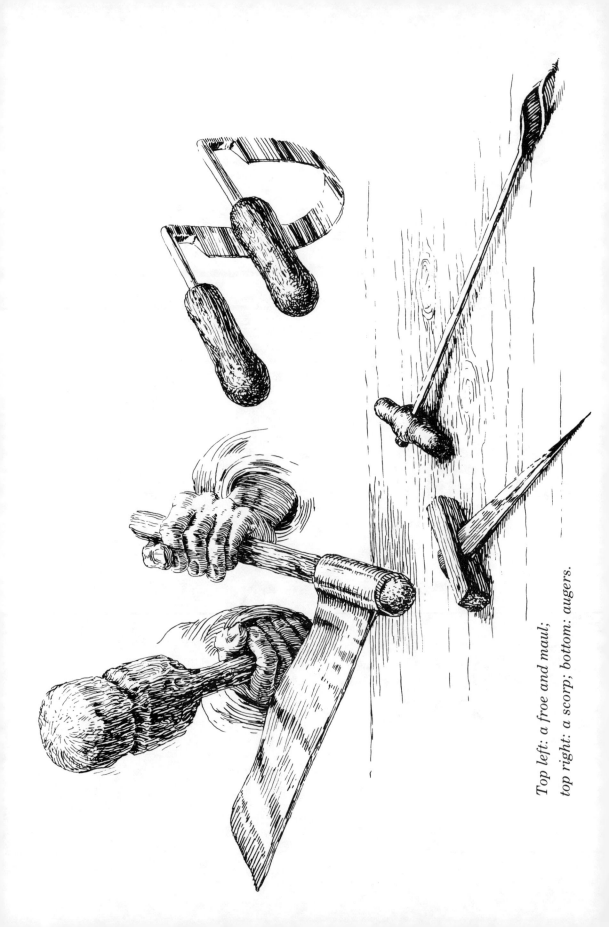

*Top left: a froe and maul;
top right: a scorp; bottom: augers.*

When he needed a new tool he often made it himself, sometimes inventing a tool to fit a particular job.

Farmers arriving in the wilderness brought along oxen, or horses, or any other livestock they owned and could move. The poorer families often arrived on foot, and without animals. First, they purchased a cow. The cow gave milk for the children and provided butter for the entire family. Rich, yellow cream rose to the top of milk, as it cooled in crocks in the springhouse. This cream was skimmed off, and when there was enough, it was churned into butter. What remained in the crock was buttermilk, which was served with corn dodgers.

Because there was no pasture for the cow that came to the frontier, she was allowed to graze on the grass and brush in the woods around the clearing. At night, she was kept inside a fence built of logs or split rails, or she was tied to a stake or post until the settler found time to build fences.

Around the little clearing, there were also a few chickens and geese. Most of these barnyard birds came west with the settlers, who needed the eggs and meat, and who would eventually use the goose feathers to fill their mattresses.

The settler's hogs foraged in the woods. These lanky animals were known for their long snouts and mean dispositions. They had long legs that carried them through the woods so fast they were known as "wind splitters." The animals were a match for any predator met in the woods except wolves, that stole young pigs from their mothers. The hogs were also called "elm peelers," because if other wild foods were scarce, they ate the roots of the slippery elm and other plants. They also fed on acorns and anything else they could find, including snakes and the eggs of ground nesting birds. The settlers said these wood-ranging hogs "could do everything but climb trees." They sometimes became so wild, the settler could not mark or brand them; he could only catch them with the help of his rifle.

The settlers needed wool for clothing, and as soon as they could, they had sheep brought west to them. The sheep arrived after frontier farmers had cleared their land, built their cabins, and trapped enough furbearing animals to barter for the sheep.

Nearly every family owned a pack of dogs that guarded the livestock from bears and wolves, gave warning of the approach of Indians, and hunted with their master.

A settler often worked into the evening. He labored outside until dark. Then, by the light of the fireplace or candles, he mended harnesses or made shoes for his family. He retired early, and the following morning was up before dawn and at his work again.

Not all settlers were this ambitious, however. Some, who scarcely worked at all, lived in unimproved cabins throughout their lives, surviving by hunting and trapping. But most settlers cleared their land, replaced their cabins with log houses, helped build schools and churches, and watched changes come swiftly to the frontier.

6

Wild Animals and Hunting

The first settlers to come into the wilderness mixed farming with hunting. Clearing land took a long time, and until the farmer could plant and harvest crops for food, he frequently lifted his long rifle from its pegs and told his wife he was going in search of game.

His chances of finding game were excellent, especially in the early years. He hunted wild turkeys, quail, plover, prairie chickens, woodcock, heath hens, coots, rails, passenger pigeons, Eskimo curlews, and many kinds of wild geese and ducks. He also killed deer, elks, bison, bears, rabbits, squirrels, raccoons, beavers, and opossums.

The settler was usually an expert shot, skilled with a gun since boyhood. Boys who lived in frontier block houses and pioneer homes learned the skills of the Indians. They discovered how to recognize the barking of the gray squirrel, and the call of the turkey gobbler in spring. And they learned to walk quietly in the deep shadows and surprise a bird or a squirrel. At the age of twelve or thirteen, the frontier boy was given a rifle and shot pouch. He took pride in his shooting, his woodsman-

63

ship, and his ability to bring home wild game for the family table.

Giant wild turkeys lived from the Atlantic coast to Missouri and from Florida to Ontario. They weighed twenty or more pounds, and were often in flocks. The first settlers sometimes found turkeys near their clearings. The sharp-eyed turkeys stepped lightly through the forest, searching the ground for acorns, nuts, insects, and roots. The settlers shot them with their rifles, but they also learned turkey-hunting tricks from the Indians. One of these methods was to bait wild turkeys into traps. The settler started by building a log pen in the forest. Then, he dug a narrow trench under one side of the pen. When this was ready, he dropped a line of yellow, shelled corn through the forest. The trail of corn led to the enclosure. Turkeys, picking up the grains, went into the trench, then up into the pen. They did not escape because they only looked up at the covered top of the pen, not down where the trench was.

In the spring, a skilled hunter could call the big turkey gobblers to him. From the hollow wing bone of the turkey, he fashioned a special horn, on which he made calls that sounded like a turkey hen. Then, before daylight, the hunter went to the woods and waited near where the old turkey gobbler was on his roost, high up in a tree. As the gobbler came off the roost, the hunter imitated the calls of the female turkey. The strutting gobbler came closer and closer, all the while filling the woods with the rolling sound of his gobbling.

At other times, the hunter waited in the woods, hidden behind a pile of brush, until the feeding turkeys came in range of his gun.

Whenever he could, the hunter killed deer—found everywhere in the early days of settlement. A deer would feed the hunter's family for days, and there were a dozen uses for the hide.

The settler understood the whitetail deer of eastern North America. He learned that nature had given it a sense of hearing

A wild turkey.

as sharp as any creature in the woods. If a hunter stepped on a twig, a deer a quarter of a mile away would hear the twig snap. And the animal's delicate and sensitive nose detected signs of danger carried on the wind. But the hunter also knew of the deer's poor eyesight. By standing still, at the edge of the woods, he knew that a deer might come so close he could reach out and slap it, if it failed to hear or smell him.

The skilled deer hunter made use of this information. He went through the woods, watching for the large tracks the deer left in the mud. He found where the tracks came together at the crossing of a creek or in the middle of a ridge. He knew that the deer would be feeding at night, and that during the day-time they hid in the thick brush—sleeping lightly and resting, but always ready to bound to their feet and dash away if an enemy came close.

In early morning or late evening, when the deer were moving from their beds to their feeding places, the hunter waited by their trail. Choosing his hiding place upwind, he crouched in the brush, or sat by the base of a big tree until a deer moved into range.

Old records tell of settlers taking deer at night by using flares. Floating down a small stream, a hunter in the front of a canoe carried a flaming pine knot. The light blinded the curious deer, coming to the water's edge to drink, and the animal stood and stared at it.

The species of animals hunted depended on the area in which the settlers lived. Those who lived in the prairies hunted antelope and prairie chickens. Some fed their families much of the year on jack rabbits. Other settlers lived where ducks and geese came through in fall by the thousands, and returned in spring, as they migrated north again.

Wild pigeons—the now extinct passenger pigeon—crossed the skies in flocks so thick, they shaded the forests from the sun. Millions of them came into view in the distance, like smoke on the horizon. They rushed on until the roaring of their wings filled the air. The settlers soon learned that these birds were good to eat.

Shooting pigeons was slow work, and bullets were costly. A quicker way to kill them was to stretch a big net over an open area in the forest, and spread grain beneath the net until the pigeons grew accustomed to eating there. Then, when the feeding pigeons covered the ground, the settler, hidden in the brush, pulled a string. This caused the net to drop over dozens of the birds.

Pigeon hunters even found the birds' roosts and used sticks to knock the pigeons out of the trees at night. There were times when pigeon hunters sold the birds at twenty-five cents a bushel.

Of all the wild animals that contributed their furs to the frontier people, none was more important than the beaver. Known for its flat tail, sharp teeth, and rich brown fur, the animal paddled about the ponds and streams of the wilderness, digging into banks, and cutting down trees for its food. It changed the landscape by building dams and backing the water up into pools.

The settlers shipped beaver fur to the East, where it was sold. But first the beaver had to be captured, and this demanded a high level of skill on the part of the trapper. The successful beaver trapper won the respect of people in the community because he understood the ways of the animal. An old account tells us how the animals were trapped:

The trapper, searching for signs of the beaver's presence, watched for tracks in the mud. He looked for the bits of green wood the beaver sometimes left floating on the water. Willow, birch, and aspen were beaver favorites. The trapper also searched for recently cut trees. These signs told him where the animals were, and he prepared to set his traps.

He had to be careful to hide his own tracks and not let the beaver smell the man scent. Traveling in a canoe helped. Or if he had no canoe, the trapper waded upstream instead of walk-

Setting beaver traps.

ing on the bank. When he located the spot where beaver were going in and out of the water, he set the open jaws of the steel trap near the water's edge, three inches below the surface.

Next, he cut a stick and put one end of it in the ground above the trap. The top of the stick reached into the air, above the trap, and the end of this stick was covered with a special scent the trapper made to attract the beaver's attention. The scent was a mixture of the beaver's scent gland, blended with a liquid made by boiling the roots and bark of spicebush. The beaver, reaching for the scented end of the young branch, would put one foot into the trap.

The trapper had a chain attached to the trap, and the chain was tied to a rope made from the twisted bark of leatherwood. The trapped beaver had line enough to drag the trap into deep water and there, if the trapper's plan worked, the animal drowned quickly.

By setting a string of these traps, a skilled trapper could collect enough beaver hides to make $300 or $400 in a few months. This was big money on the frontier, where cash was rare.

During certain years, squirrels became so numerous that thousands of them ran through the woods and over the fields in a huge migration, eating the farmers' crops as they went. In 1807, in southern Ohio, for example, squirrels swarmed across the Ohio River from Kentucky. Some, swept away by the current, drowned, but most seemed to succeed in crossing the stream and invading the settlers' fields.

The Ohio state legislature quickly passed a law, demanding that every taxpayer kill and turn in from ten to one hundred squirrels a year. If they failed to kill their quota of squirrels, farmers were fined three cents for each squirrel they were short. But nature took care of the surplus. The following winter was bitterly cold, and the squirrels became so rare, the settlers could not find any to kill. The new bounty law on squirrels was quickly forgotten.

On the frontier, there was a deep hatred of wolves—large, powerful animals that roamed the forests in packs. Whenever farm families talked of wolves, fear filled their voices. From the time they were young, children heard stories of wolves attacking people.

If a hunter encountered a pack of wolves, he told his neighbors, and they told others. Each time the story was repeated, the wolves seemed to become more fierce. Old writings tell of people being held at bay all night by packs of wolves that circled them tirelessly, until dawn brought rescue. Other stories, possibly exaggerated, tell of wolves driving hunters into trees and keeping them there until rescued.

Wolves were considered to be such enemies of farmers that states often passed laws to encourage people to kill them. Illinois offered a $200 prize to the person killing the greatest number of wolves during seven months of 1824. But to win this prize, the person had to kill at least 60 wolves. At the same time, there was a $20 prize for the champion wolf killer in each Illinois county, if the winner killed at least 10 wolves.

Even more feared than the wolves was the giant cat we call a cougar, or mountain lion, and the pioneer called a panther, or painter. As quickly as they could, farmers and hunters killed off the cougars. There was no longer room for these predators in a land being tamed by settlers and stocked with domestic animals.

Black bears that lived in the forests were both a problem and a boon. The flesh of the bear provided meat, and the fat was used for cooking and for dressing leather. The bear's heavy black fur was used on the pioneer's bed. But these large animals, plodding through the shadowed forests, were a challenge. Each man and boy considered it his duty to kill every bear he could. The killing of a bear gave a hunter status, and if he was a good bear hunter, this was known for miles around.

Nowhere was the bear safe. One Ohio settler spotted a bear swimming in a river. The man's gun was in his cabin, but

his boat was on the shore. He pushed the boat into the stream, planning to keep the bear in deep water until it drowned. The bear, however, began climbing into the boat. The hunter had to climb out the other side. The last the settler saw of the animal, it was drifting around a bend in the river, riding comfortably in the hunter's boat.

Bears killed the farmers' hogs and sheep, knocked over the bee hives, and stole the honey. A settler, discovering his loss, put aside his field work and called his hounds. The dogs were used for trailing foxes, raccoons, wild hogs, bears, and deer. If the hounds picked up the trail of a bear, they chased it until it climbed a tree to get away from them. Then the dogs held it there, howling steadily, until the hunter, huffing and puffing, arrived with his gun.

To the settlers coming into the wilderness, there must have seemed no end to the wildlife. What they needed they took, and the wild game they hunted helped them live through those first hard years. Sometimes their diet was nearly all meat. Even when they raised hogs, they continued to hunt deer, bears, and turkeys. The settlers lived close to nature, and wild animals were part of the wilderness around them.

Wherever they went, the settlers changed the land—for the wild creatures as well as for themselves. The trees vanished to make room for corn and wheat. As the home of the forest game vanished, the animals disappeared. The deer no longer had the woodlands through which they once walked and gathered their food. The bears no longer had a place to live.

The wild turkeys were gone from Connecticut by 1813 and from Massachusetts by 1851. There were none left in Ohio by 1878. They disappeared from 19 of the 36 states where the birds once lived. They had been both over-hunted and robbed of their habitats.

The forests have since come back on much of the land. As the trees return, the forest wildlife may also come back. There are deer in the woods again, and with them, some wild turkeys. But the passenger pigeons will never return. They are extinct.

7

What the Settlers Wore

Those who lived in the eastern cities could buy their shoes from a cobbler's shop and clothing from a tailor. But frontier clothing was not easy to obtain.

When people moved west into the wilderness, they took along extra clothing, if they could afford it, or cloth for making more clothes. Some travelers owned only what they wore, and heavy work and the rough life soon wore out their clothes. They then had to find materials from which to make more clothing. They had only one choice. Like the Indians and the frontier hunters, the earliest settlers made clothes from the skins of wild animals.

Shoes were a special problem. The first settlers often wore deerskin moccasins like those the Indians wore. They were almost knee-high, and when the weather turned cold, they were lined with deerhair for insulation.

Before too long, however, pioneering families became shoemakers, as well as farmers and hunters.

The fresh animal hides were called "green skins," because nothing had been done to them. Deerskin had to be treated to make it soft, useful, and durable. This process started with drying the brains from the deer on a board propped in front of the fireplace. The dried deer brains were then wrapped in a piece of cloth, while a kettle of water warmed in the fireplace. The cloth, holding the deer brains, was swished vigorously in the warm water, until there were light suds. Next, the hide was dropped into the water and rubbed until it was thoroughly wet. Then it was lifted from the kettle, and the water was squeezed from it.

The pioneer stretched the wet skin over a board to clean it and work on it, then left it there to dry. Then he added more brains to the water, and washed the deerskin in the mixture again. Once more, the skin was stretched over the board; then it was worked back and forth until it became soft.

The final step was to hang the deerskin where the smoke from a hickory fire would flow over it. The smoke helped cure the skin and keep it from rotting.

When the treated deer hide was ready for the settler's wife to fashion into clothing, she used a butcher knife to cut the skin to the pattern she wanted. Instead of using a paper pattern, as the modern seamstress might, the pioneer woman guessed at measurements and cut the garment to fit loosely. She punched holes in the edges of the pieces with an awl, and sewed the pieces together with the tough sinews from the leg of a deer.

Deerskin clothing did not keep a person dry in the rain. When it became soaked, then had dried again, it often became hard as wood. One frontiersman told how it felt to pull on a pair of these trousers on a cold winter morning. He said that if the trousers were dropped on the floor, they rattled like kettles. And when a man pulled them on, it felt as if he were sticking his legs into a pair of stove pipes.

The only way to keep buckskin soft, if it became wet, was to work it constantly as it dried. But skin clothing did have advantages. It formed a good windbreaker. It was sound protection against briars and thorns, and snakes had trouble biting through it.

Skins served the settlers until they had wool for spinning and weaving.

Then the men built spinning wheels for their wives, and the spinning became a job that kept women and girls busy much of the time. At first, they spun wool from the hair of wild animals, especially the buffalo. Some also attempted to weave the hair of the black bear into cloth. But these materials do not twist as does sheep's wool.

Sometimes the women sent the children into the fields to gather milkweed heads. These fluffy fibers, that carry the seeds on the wind, were combined with buffalo wool and made into cloth, but it was a coarse, low-quality material. Women who had worked fine sheep's wool back in the East, longed for wool, and before the family had been many years on the frontier, sheep were being brought west to the settlers.

In spring, men and boys caught the sheep and cut off the layer of wool with scissor-like shears. In the wool were burrs and dirt, and these foreign materials had to be picked out by hand. The next step was carding—a process that made the wool fibers ready for spinning. Carding was done with a pair of flat hand-tools with numerous pointed spikes, or wires, sticking up from them. One was pulled across the other to straighten the fibers and prepare them for the spinning wheel. Because carding was a tedious job, settlements soon had people going into business operating carding mills. Farmers from miles around brought their wool for this time-consuming step in the cloth making process.

Using spinning wheels, hour after hour, the women and girls turned the wool into yarn. It was then bleached, perhaps also dyed, before being woven into cloth. Work and hunting clothes, however, were seldom bleached or dyed.

The settlers used one other important source of fibers for making clothes. After they had cleared enough land and were

Carding wool.

growing food for themselves and their livestock, they planted a small patch of flax. Late in the summer, its pretty blue flowers would bend in the soft winds that swept over the farm. But the settler's wife knew that ahead lay long hours of hard work before the flax could be woven into cloth. Flax is an ancient crop; its seed is used for making linseed oil, which today is used in making paints, oilcloth, and other products. But the early settler planted it mostly for the long strong fibers growing just beneath the outer surface, around the woody core of the stem.

As the plants ripened, the first job was to pull the whole plant from the ground. The settlers sometimes had flax-pulling parties. Young people would ride off on their horses to their neighbors to pull up the flax, and then stay to dance.

The next step was to remove the seeds. This was called "rippling," and was done with special combs that separated the seeds from the plant. Then came "retting," or soaking the stems in water to separate the fibers from the woody part of the flax plant. When the stalks had dried, they were ready for "breaking." The settlers held the flax stalks, a handful at a time, across the narrow edge of a board, and beat the plants with mallets to break the woody parts into smaller pieces. The final step was "scutching," in which stalks were whacked and scraped between two boards to free the fibers. The long, fine fibers were separated from the shorter ones, which were coarse, but nevertheless were used for making work clothes to be worn in summertime. Or they were woven into ropes or twine.

What was left now were the "line" fibers, and these were woven into the family's best clothing. The cloth woven from this fine material was bleached white in the sun. Pioneer women spread the linen in the sun, moistened it every hour or so, and allowed it to dry. They repeated this process until the cloth was a beautiful, almost pure white. If streaks of gray remained in the linen cloth, frontier people seldom worried about it, unless they needed cloth for Sunday clothes or wedding dresses.

Common flax.

A flax-scutching bee.

The settlers also made cloth by weaving wool and flax fibers together, and this material was called "linsey-woolsey."

Modern people seldom give a second thought to where buttons for their clothing will come from, but buttons were a problem for the settlers. Flax thread was sometimes wrapped into buttons for linen shirts. At other times, buttons were made by sewing a piece of cloth over a small piece of wood.

Pioneer women knew how to dye their cloth with natural materials. The hulls of walnuts would turn cloth dark brown. Ripe pokeberries gave it a crimson color. If a settler's wife wanted green cloth, she dyed it with peach leaves. For yellow, she used smartweed.

Even the best clothes owned by the settlers were often rough and scratchy. For this reason, they were sometimes soaked in warm water and beaten until the material became softer.

Early settlers had few clothes. What they owned, they hung on pegs on their cabin walls. There might be an extra dress for each daughter, and an extra pair of trousers for each boy. There were heavier wool clothes for winter, and lighter linens or linsey-woolsey for warmer weather. As settlers became more prosperous, their wardrobes included special dress clothes for weddings, churchgoing, or courting on Sunday afternoons.

But for the early settlers, clothes first of all had to be practical. There was seldom cloth enough for making underwear. Shoes and boots were the same for the left foot as the right. Men at work seldom wore socks. In summer the women wore sunbonnets and everyday dresses of linsey-woolsey, made in one piece to slip over the head. Around the neck was a drawstring.

Children's clothing would be handed down to younger members of a family as long as the garments held together. In the settler's world, there was no time to waste nor materials to be thrown away if a use could be found for them.

8

Keeping Clean and Healthy

Frontier life was for the rugged and the healthy. The weak were weeded out by disease and carried off to family burying grounds. People were not surprised when they caught flu, mumps, measles, or whooping cough, or when they contracted sore eyes and skin diseases. These problems came with living. Nobody understood how easy they were making it for diseases to spread.

It was difficult to keep the settler's home clean. Soap was made at home and carefully allotted. When the kettle in the fireplace was used for cooking venison stew, there was no way it could be used to heat water for scrubbing. The men worked in the fields and barnyards, and mud and manure clung to their boots and trousers. Their wives also worked outdoors as well as inside.

Clothes were seldom washed. Neither were bodies. Men and boys, if they bathed at all, washed in a creek or pond when the weather was warm. Otherwise, there could only be the bath from a basin, placed before the fire. Everyone washed from the same basin, and dried his or her hands and face on the same

85

towel. There might be one comb for the family; nobody had toothbrushes. Sometimes people cleaned their teeth with a bit of salt on a damp rag. More often, teeth received no special care, and many a settler went toothless into old age. There was the common water bucket filled with drinking water from a creek or spring. Beside it hung a gourd or tin cup, from which everyone drank. The crossroads store had its own water bucket and cup, as did the schoolhouse. The sick drank and left germs for the next in line.

Insects—part of farm living—were also abundant in the early villages. There seemed to be little that could be done about these pests. There were no screens for doors or windows; flies flitted from milk crocks to honey jars and, in summer, filled the home with their constant buzzing. The women kept a small branch handy to brush away flies and other insects if they became too thick.

Because they could not keep clean, the settlers were often sick. They had arrived at the frontier at a time when medical science was young, and they did not understand how germs grew or spread, or even that germs existed. People did not, for example, know how typhoid fever could spread so rapidly through the settlements, striking down entire families. They were not aware that the organism causing this disease was carried in the wastes from the bodies of afflicted people and polluted water supplies. Not until about 1835 did doctors begin to understand that typhoid was a disease; until then, there was little anyone could do to help its victims. Historians believe that many frontier deaths, attributed to other causes, were really caused by typhoid.

Among the most common and debilitating of all frontier ailments was the "ague." Some said it was not really a sickness, but a part of life on the frontier. A person might work hard in the fields or woods from sun-up to sunset, and feel fine all day. The next day, a chill might come upon him and cause him to shake so hard his teeth would clatter together. After the "shakes" passed, he might become warm again, then burn with fever. He would also have severe head and muscle pains. Then the spell would vanish, and the victim would recover. But once a person caught the disease, it lasted for years and could flare up every few days.

People knew that the ague seemed to strike harder at those who lived in low swampy areas. But they did not understand why. In the blood of the victim lived a single-celled organism, a parasite. Before it could complete its life cycle, it had to live in the body of a certain mosquito, the female *Anopheles*. The mosquitos, buzzing around the settlers in their cabins at night, were more than a nuisance. They flew from person to person spreading the ague, or what is now called malaria.

Medicines, used to fight the disease, were gathered from the woods and fields. The settlers tried everything the doctors suggested, including tea made of sassafras or of mullen plants that grew in the pastures. One doctor recommended killing a chicken and holding its body against the soles of the feet. Another recommended swallowing cobwebs, rolled into a ball.

Doctors were rare among the settlers. Sickness was treated by family members or by neighbors. A settler's wife was the family specialist in treating sickness and disease. If there was a doctor, he was called in, only in serious emergencies. He might have to come a long distance on horseback, and there was seldom money in the settler's home to pay him. The doctors were often paid in chickens, eggs, or meat.

Few doctors who worked the frontier settlements had been to a medical school. At best, a doctor might have served three years apprenticeship with a practicing doctor. He had assisted the doctor in all his tasks, and had learned to bandage wounds. He had also practiced mixing medicines because early doctors mixed their own, often with raw materials carried in their saddlebags.

Gradually, the medical student learned the skills of his master. When the time came, the doctor certified that his stu-

dent was ready to be called "doctor" and begin his own prac-
tice. He performed surgery and pulled teeth, set bones, and
treated patients for the most serious diseases. There were also
those who had no training at all, but who practiced medicine
and called themselves "doctors."

Long before European settlers arrived, the Indians had
their own medicine men and medicines made of herbs and
other natural materials. Some of these medicines had been
used for thousands of years, and several of the Indian cures—
his herbs and compounds—were adopted by the settlers. Meanwhile, the settler's wife brought her own ideas, and those of her
mother and grandmother to the task of caring for her sick
family.

People who did not know how to treat sickness often relied

Bitten by a rattlesnake.

on superstitions. A pioneer mother might tie the foot of a mole on a string and hang it around her baby's neck, believing this made it easier for the baby's first teeth to come through. The baby's father, meanwhile, might carry a seed from the buckeye tree in his pocket, thinking this made his rheumatism less painful.

Another frontier superstition said only the "madstone" could save a person bitten by a mad dog. Someone bitten by a rabid animal was rushed to the home of anyone who owned a madstone, said to have been taken from the stomach of a white deer. It was believed to have a magic power that drew poison from the body of the victim. Those bitten often believed that if they could not get to a madstone, they would surely catch the disease, go mad, foam at the mouth and begin biting everyone

around them. There was a joke along the frontier that if you were bitten by a mad dog, and couldn't get to a madstone, you had better make your will. Then you could make a list of folks you wanted to bite.

Snakebite was also sometimes a problem. The story is told of two frontier boys, eight and six years old, working one summer day in their father's tobacco field. When the younger boy placed his hand on the base of a tobacco plant, he suddenly cried out that he had been bitten by a rattlesnake. He then ordered his brother to cut off the hand to save his life. The only tool available was a dull tomahawk. The six-year-old boy laid his hand on a stump. His brother was unable to do the job, but after a little hesitation, he cut off the finger the snake had bitten. It is said that the boy survived and grew to manhood, always reminded by that missing finger of the day he was bitten.

9

Frontier Recreation

We have come to think that the early pioneers were loners, who would rather be by themselves than with other people. There were people like this—Daniel Boone and nameless settlers who stayed in their own hollows and preferred to be left alone. But most people welcomed the opportunity to visit with their neighbors. In early settlements, miles of wilderness separated the backwoods family from the nearest humans. Almost any excuse was a reason for lonely pioneers to get together.

The settler, who had cut trees to clear his land, sent out word through the neighborhood for all to come to the logrolling. On the appointed day, people came from miles around because they themselves would need help someday, and this was a labor-sharing event. But they also came because of the fun. The day of work was long and hard. Heavy logs had to be moved, piled high, and burned to ashes. From dawn to dusk, they worked and sweated. The whiskey jug was nearly always at hand, because whiskey was considered an important part of the settlers' life.

Wives, too, came to the logrolling. They brought food and

their favorite recipes. They were busy throughout the day, exchanging gossip while they cooked and tended babies. When the logs were rolled and the fires from them still glowed in the clearing, the men came from the field for supper. But the day was not yet done. The settlers who had worked all day were now ready to play well into the night. Old folks might start for home after the evening meal, but the young people stayed for the fiddle-playing and dancing.

In the fall, corn had to be husked. The settler pulled the ears from the stalks, hauled them into the barn, and dumped them in a pile on the floor. Again, word went out through the settlement: "Come Thursday evening, there will be a husking bee at Deaver's place." After a day of work on their own farms, the people headed for the husking bee. Both men and women came—especially the young people. Husking corn was gentle work that brought people close together. Working shoulder to shoulder, they exchanged jokes and gossip as they husked.

Almost any event on the frontier was turned into a contest. Two captains were chosen for the husking bee. Then each captain selected his team. This meant that the pile of corn in the middle of the barn floor had to be divided in half. A long rail was laid on top of the pile, and worked down through the middle, until the corn separated into two piles. These piles were moved far enough apart to let people kneel at their husking. Then the two teams, back to back, began husking at the same moment.

Each man carried his own husking peg—a sharpened piece of wood, held in the palm of the hand by a leather strap that fit around the fingers. He stuck the point of the husking peg through the tip of the brown husks, in which the ear of corn was wrapped. With a sharp jerk of both hands, he stripped the husk from each long ear of yellow corn and broke it off at the base of the ear. The team hit its stride and developed a rhythm, and yellow ears flew through the air into a pile that grew as the evening wore on.

A corn-husking bee.

If a fortunate young settler found that he had suddenly husked an ear of corn that was red, the rules said he could kiss the girl of his choice. More than one young man carried a red ear from home in his pocket.

Almost any big seasonal job could be tackled by the same group plan. Before apples could be dried, they had to be peeled, and apple paring was another excuse for neighborhood young people to get together.

Logrollings, cornhuskings, wood choppings, apple parings, church meetings, and dances gave young people the opportunity to congregate. Much of the recreation on the frontier was rough by nature—reflecting the settlers' rugged lives and the constant need to prove their strength in the wilderness. In this atmosphere, a man's gun was always close. Even when he no longer had to hunt for food, the settler was proud of his shooting skills. Wherever a few men gathered, a shooting match might develop. Often, this meant shooting at a small target at 75 or 100 yards, with the shooters betting on who would score best.

The settlers' children had their own games and toys, including homemade sleds and small wagons. Boys made themselves bows and arrows, as well as slings, and became skilled in their use. They whittled whistles from the branches of willow trees, and they fished with cane poles and worms. In fall, boys and girls gathered hickory nuts, walnuts, and hazelnuts. During long winter nights, the family members cracked the nuts on the hearth and popped corn over the coals. There were also neighborhood spelling bees in which both adults and children took part.

It was at these special events, and at church meetings, that young people met. There were shy glances, hand holding, and sometimes riding home from a dance together. The settlement knew who was "keeping company," and folks were usually not surprised when word of a forthcoming wedding was carried through the neighborhood. A wedding was a celebra-

tion for an entire settlement. When the day arrived, friends of the groom came to his home to escort him to the bride's home.

The groom was often dressed in a new suit, made especially for his wedding. His bride might wear a dress worn years earlier by her mother back East, and carefully brought west for this special day. Or if they did not have, and could not obtain, these special wedding clothes, the bride wore a homemade dress of linsey-woolsey and the groom also wore an outfit made of homespun cloth.

Dishes were borrowed for the occasion, and outdoor tables were set up. Women in the settlement came to help cook the wild game and pork and bake pies and corn bread.

The ceremony was usually short and simple, read either by a minister, if one could be found, or by a justice of the peace. Afterwards, when the women cooked the food, the men engaged in the games of skill popular on the frontier. They included running, jumping, wrestling, throwing the tomahawk, or shooting at a mark.

By evening, the women had cleared the tables. The young people, however, and perhaps most of the older ones, too, stayed for dancing and games that continued into the night. But this was not the end of the celebration. The following day, the party began all over again. During this second day, known as the "infair," guests ate another grand meal and again danced far into the night.

10

The Changing Frontier

Some of the things the settlers needed, they could not make. For many settlers, however, there were no stores, so they waited for the peddler to come down the road. When he stopped in a dusty lane before a log house, the family gathered around. Cash was scarce, but the peddler would accept chickens, pigs, and even garden crops in exchange for his goods. Some peddlers started in business by walking with a pack over their shoulders. If they made good, they bought a horse, then a wagon or buggy, and, later, even a store as the village grew.

There were not many ways settlers could raise cash. Instead of exchanging money for goods, they bartered. They traded furs for salt or coffee. They roamed the forests in late summer and early autumn months, searching for ginseng—a small woodland plant with red berries. The roots have been used for medicines, especially by Oriental people, for hundreds of years. Ginseng can still be found in the forest today, but it has become very rare. Pioneers dug the plants and dried the roots and sold them at the store in the settlement.

Another product the early farmers sold for cash was the

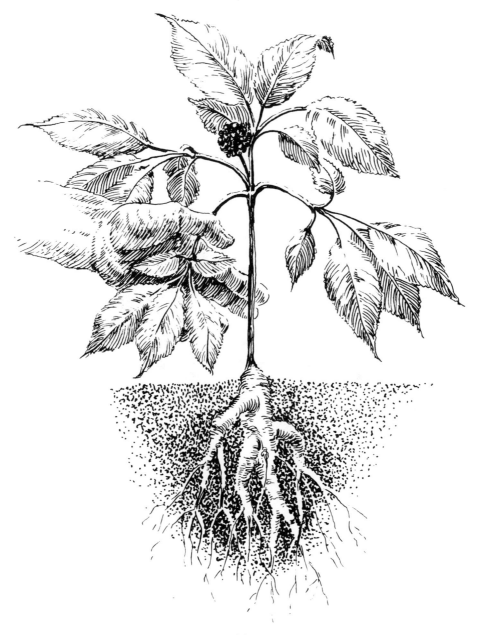

Ginseng.

ashes from the fires that burned the fallen trees. Back in the eastern states and in Europe, this potash was used for making soap and in the manufacturing of glass. The earliest news-papers ran advertisements by merchants, offering to buy wood ashes. Settlers were advised to save the ashes in sheds on wooden floors, that would protect them from the elements until enough had been collected to bring them in for sale. Both the wood ashes from the fields, where the logs were burned, and those accumulating in the family fireplace could be marketed.

As the settlers' farms prospered and the farmers produced more grain than they needed for their own families, they searched for ways to sell it for cash. Their major grain was corn, and most of it went into the making of hominy, mush, and corn bread for the family table or for the farmer's live-stock. But if there was any corn left, it was frequently made into whiskey, which could be easily shipped and sold. But when the settlements grew, and the demand for meat in the frontier towns increased, farmers began feeding their corn to hogs, which they eventually drove to town to sell. In time, also, the farm wife made extra money by selling eggs from her flock of chickens.

The frontier changed rapidly. Within a single lifetime, the giant trees and wild game vanished from much of the land. Successful farmers grew prosperous, and their homes grew bigger. Other settlers found new professions. Lawyers and preachers, who had ridden circuits, moved to thriving towns to set up permanent quarters in offices and churches. Railroads, canalboats, and steamboats brought goods from distant places. People could buy what they needed.

The land the settlers had opened changed for all time. Few people remembered the frontier days, when their fathers and grandfathers tackled the wilderness with axes, oxen, and a yearning for land of their own.

INDEX

INDEX